ALREADY THERE

Poems

by

S.D. HILDERBRAND

Inverspace Press
Austin, Texas

Already There:
a collection of poems longing to find home.

All poems written in Austin, TX, except:

Prattsburg, NY:
"Prattsburg, Summer"
"Crow Hill Autumn"

Chesapeake, VA:
"Frames"

Santa Cruz, CA:
"Highway 17"

St. Michaels, MD:
"Between the scales & bones"

Assembled December 2011
Austin, TX (home for now)

Photo cover taken by the author in St. Lucia.

ISBN: 978-1-300-26244-2

"Hill Country Winter" was first published in *Inverspace Quarterly* in 2009.

For Kristin

Contents

2010

Passing on
The last time

2011

News
buildup
Shadows by Lamplight
Highway 17
Between the scales & bones
Estuary
cybo (death by translation)
Morte

2007

HOME, OF A PAST LIFE

Home, those hollow halls
within each memory's loss
and a faint echo
another passing shadow
across a mortared wall.

Moss grows laterally
along the bare retainer
clings to life
and the raindrops pirouette
in an old rusty drum.

The iron container
above which a meniscus
clings to life
drops discuss in concentric
waves our reflection.

Flat discus wavers
over the shallow resonance
and a faint echo
in the deep pool
of a past life.

SOME OTHER DAY

I have walked
by you
a thousand times
in our house

and though
you were probably
awaiting
a sweet kiss

Forgive me
I was delirious
so young
and so old.

THIS GIFT I GIVE

This gift I give was once a thought,
Birthed from another mum
Frozen last winter;
Rain by day and ice by night
Bent the trees into arbors, laid tropicals down.

Then in spring's slumber the sun's lungs
Resuscitated one evening this seedling,
And then in summer's spring
Sun stopped the rain of seasonal will,
Another mother nursed the bud with chlorophyll.

This kiss you give, this love you let
Take root in your garden,
Raised in another country
Under a foreign philosophy
With no vase, no base, no bed to call home.

ADRIFT IN AN URBAN SEA

A plastic bag
an unfurled sail
large enough for

2 cartons of milk
a can of yams
floats in the

wind & tumbles
end over end
in the gusts

close to the ground
& around cars
buses and businessmen

then up and over
signs & signals
alone singley

soars into the waiting
arms of the branches
of a wilting tree.

I NEED A SPACE

i need a space
a place to call
my very own.

this location
lies beyond mere
speculation

provides a place
for introspection
thought collection

to find a new
direction
find a new facing.

these days
i sleep soundly
without a peep

secure in knowing
that when i die
i'll have a box

six feet long
six feet deep –
my very own space.

HILL COUNTRY WINTER

The treeline lopes with a gnawing slope
Down to the lakeline, that icy sheet
Pulled over the eyes in winter.

Then the head comes up and over
Disarming suspense with a lifting motion,
The sky a stratus staircase.

What underscores the face of every lake,
Every meandering stream that awakes,
A simple reflection that climbs into the dawn,

Burrowing in a bed of delicate moments
Which bloom in the light and wilt by nightfall,
This is the heart of Texas after all.

CATCH A TIGER BY THE TONGUE

once upon an evening jaunt
from down inside an unknown swamp
i came across a striped feline
which made for me a right beeline.

with obtuse fangs in mighty pangs
and anise in his pounce,
he shaked his head quite fussily,
but must have weighed an ounce

too much or more the branch he left,
bereft of hue, it snapped in two,
and cleft just like a sentence through.
but deftly did the tiger up

and found me so alone, hopped down
and pounced upon his little snack.
i hope you didn't want me back –
you'll never get me home again.

so if perchance you come upon
a tiger of your own,
do unlike me the wiser thing,
and leave that cat alone!

THE BEFORE AND THE AFTER

He was never concerned
with how things had been.
As the ash dangled over
the precipice of his fingers
his snore caught a chortle
emerging from dream's portal,
he spoke of future memories
dreams of retirement travels
that lingered in the closed-up
basement like second-hand smoke.

Rising from his recliner,
taking an angle from late night
broadcasts of Larry King
from a timezone six hours
behind the ticking clock,
the second hand counting down
his days left to pass.

He rarely spoke of the past,
always the impending soon
beyond misty Bavarian mornings
fantasied as our ancestral home
drinking the amber lager
that ran down in barrels
tapping out oompah, the opas
in pheasant feathers and caps
the frothy mugs and beards
in the shadow of the Alps.

2008

FOR KRISTIN

The last time I saw you
we shared a dinner off a slingshot,
then curled up with our pillows
like willows in winter –

I massaged the day off your body
and the light was like a t.v. mosaic
of seltzer bubbles in my fleeting
fling with a Tom Collins –

Your hands reminded me
of a comb across a balding head,
the careful caress of your nails
like club soda fizzling flat.

After those long summer days at work
I imagined some nights you dreamed of
Kindergartens and Christkindlmarkts
under Allemagne skies.

I will give you, and you me, a child
and we'll waltz through Marienplatz,
like two marionettes in tune
with strings untangled from today.

MONDAY MORNING

The tiles in the kitchen
have warped and cracked,
attacked by too much expansion,
too many contractions,
too many breakfasts in flames.

Last night we laughed like jackals on wine
but in the morning you screamed
sirens and slammed the door,
dogs baying back under the table,
with no hope for scraps.

Your words were a sleeping dragon
startled from a century's slumber,
volcanic breath expressing
this week's frustration,
stones standing on my schedule.

Why couldn't I trade time for dinner?

Too many starts of fights
and ends of loaves of bread,
compliments cut
short
by loathsome crusts
burnt
by your anger
crumbled to dust and crumbs,
falling

apart like weekends
that rush by like menus
said all in one breath.

20-20

You haven't known humility
until you've had your foot run over
by a woman in a wheelchair
smoking an off-brand cigarette.
She rolled off as I stood in the middle
of the crosswalk and she flicked her butt
to the pavement without a single glance

To know this humility, like knotted seaweed,
those emotions that stumble over grace,
you must sit in Veggie Heaven
on the Drag in the off-peak shadows
for hours and watch the window
as the pane is passed over by hand-holding lovers
(flicking butts without a single glance)
and study your reflection in palimpsest.

In this position, you'll notice
someone's aging mother with arthritis
ambling on cloudy sandals
with a lone tray of leftovers
tossing rice to pigeons (in Tok Pisin
muttering a prayer for the many starving people
on the islands of Melanesia you'll never know)
which crumbles on the parched pavement
in the shape of Indonesia

Why do you care to notice?
Because at the far table
beyond the edge of your known world

the Spanish-speaking busgirls
sit down after the lunch shift,
enjoying an energetic picnic
in the empty restaurant,
their three voiceless whispers
echoing the cadence of confidence

Sunburnt men in their seventies
with tired rage encasing their faces
creep along the sidewalk,
mumbling to pigeons as someone's mother
hands them meals in styrofoam
(which didn't exist in their youth)
to extend time with a smile

I am the silver man from the Dobie
(the one who sweeps the floors in a stained uniform)
charging across the street
between the #1 bus and the bicycles
shielded by a black plastic bag
with all I own – a blanket, two shirts,
and the last picture of my mother before she passed
(to bury it behind a dumpster)
Though you can't help but wonder about my childhood,
how I always wanted to be in the movies,
know that my last job was Fear
and that you too will one day be ensnared as a metaphor
by some scared poet searching desperately for an image.

So go back to your uneaten
curry bun on the table,
savor it now,
and save the humble prayer

of words
for yourself.
One day they'll be all you have.

WAYPOINTS

In those autumn evenings when the sun dripped dry
we slept in the harbor, swam in our clothes.
We picked up the drunk at the liquor store, and from the
bed of your truck, he asked us
for a ride home from AA,
and then for some beer.
We left him on the corner of Wilkens and Fulton
and he popped some pills, ducked into a stoop
and out of our lives.
We never went back.

Left on Rolling Road, we pulled into U.M.B.C.
(You Made a Bad Choice we'd joke),
threw such lofty fits and storms in the dorms,
pushing each other into and out of new -isms
and your finger slammed like an apple
in the basement door, its skin
dangling from the bloody core,
and we rushed you to St. Agnes in our pajamas,
sat out front with the addicts for hours
throwing bottle caps in the birdbath.
Those ambulance sirens were little lobotomies.

Why were we so lost then?
Past the rowhomes we ran downtown,
Charm City rising in Bromoseltzer hues
And we were falling to the sidewalks like beetles
drawn in by neon letters, places with names like "BAR".
Did we want a death like Poe,
worthy only of the gutter?

Or to pass through the Blues like those other
assholes bitching about their mothers?

We rode through the streets and out to the diners,
the Double TT on Rt. 40, smoked cigarettes,
drank coffee until dawn, our books left in their bags,
wrote poems one line at a time, sharing the rhyme,
accordions of paper stained with doubt.
It's odd how in these habits,
you blink and you miss it.
We paid the bill and out in the street,
the rising sun etched its impression onto the bay.

In those days we were looking for so much more,
pacing the streets in trenchcoats,
but memory has no direction or logic.
Like the Chesapeake, only buoys light the way.

SOUFRIÈRE, ST. LUCIA, DECEMBER 2005

Under *déz Pitons*, the cinders sing with charcoal springs,
rocks ruddied with sulfur cascading down Diamond Falls,
the bearded men with carved baubles and beads,
You on vacation mahn, no pressure, no problem
mahogany straddles the stilted houses in the hills,
River Doree cool and deadly as a lady
snakes through narrow streets, pastel faded façades,
past the Church of the Assumption and central square,
childhood home of Napoleon's Empress.
The ever-windward waves,
catamarans anchor tourists just-offshore
as the wake exerts its will
on rows of canoes and buoys,
beckons like beacons to divers,
muscled men blowing conches over cruise ship horns,
parade their tuna-colored shells,
and *soté* boys from the *jump-up* in Gros Islet dive from
docks,
dreadlocks as golden as the crests of hummingbirds,
mister, madam, coin, coin! plead tourists
to throw *cent, five cent, ten cent, dollar*
into the deep water, shoving each other,
nosediving after the coins,
bodies dancing upside-down, the feet flit
like minnows, racing for the specie,
specks of silver sinking under the sea,
flipping end-over-end like the island's history –
which side you on? no pressure, no problem,
then surface and shout for more, *raison d'état,*
their voices a soca chantey, a chorus of gulls.

12 YEARS

Guilt is such a pathetic word
that nobody knows where it came from.
I had been meaning for years to talk to you,
but like a fish that's a prize from a county fair,
all I could do was sit there, gills gasping
for water, my mouth for air that's way too human
for forgiveness.
You had never approached me about it;
we always went to different schools,
and avoided each other after,
but this was our one shared cell,
a detention that would never let out.
We went to dad at Walter Reed,
watched him wither under cherry blossoms.
Why not now, when our worlds are changing?
There was a silent moment in the parking lot
between the visit
                                        and the ride home –
I chose then to confront my own illness.
You said that it was fine, but we're all affected
by what's said, what's not, and what can't be forgotten.
Damn I felt so rotten, eyes clouded with tears,
like a fish left out for a week or for years.

THE WORD

There was this foreign feeling
Encountered this cool morning;
I caught myself soaking
The marrow out of the Word

Something I thought myself
Incapable of comprehending
For the many years of my youth
Which I have somehow scored

Differently than my peers,
Marking yesterday more than tomorrow.
I sit waiting, staring at a his life-sized
Statue or more precisely, toward,

And accuracy is important
Since in this pale light
With goose pimples on my arms,
From acclimation to long summers,

I see in his shadow more
Clearly than light,
More in his dying for
Than in his life.

LEAVING THE PARISH ONE AUTUMN NIGHT

It was ten before we'd arrived,
But they had been on for a half an hour.
They only played another thirty minutes,
Long enough for just one beer,

Not even time to shake out the rust
To consider dancing.
Maybe it was the fifty people,
Maybe it was the smoking ban,

But we couldn't help but wonder
How a British once supergroup
Could end their show before eleven,
Even on a school night.

Is this what happens when we comb
Over the spots in the past?
His long hair couldn't hide how tired he sounded.
I'm glad I gave that shit up.

LIMBO OF INFANTS

November is forever falling leaves
As long as I can remember
The scattered piles of the day's labor
Undone by the icy wind
Whispering words of childhood names:
Rover, Polo, Oxen free.
Of all the seasons I prefer the autumn,
Her sacrifice
For beauty, nature will pluck the limbs of trees
Sending her children forth,
Each one a wish,
A lifetime.

These curled corpses of spring
End up on the embers of a distant fire.

2009

GRAVES OF ASHES

My father has never been laid to rest,
His name left upon no tombstone,
There is no memorial to remember him by,
Or marble to weather the ages.
More than seven years have passed,
An entire body's rebirth cell by cell,
And his ashes remain in a box on the mantle.
This obstinate stance is pitiful,
Though this vigil deserves memorial.

My shadow dog lies in the hallway
With a tumor in his spleen,
His sleeping body trembling
With the cold grasp of imminence.
He's stopped eating,
And since we cannot let him starve,
Soon Smiley will join my father
In a grave of ashes.
We've already decided it will be cremation,
To spread him in his favorite park.
He will die, then, and live in memory,
Every time we take the others to Walnut Creek.

Handsome rests his head between my akimbo arm
And hip. It's as if we're both
Refusing to let him die alone.
As evening grows quieter,
With only the scratching on the dogs and shaking of tags
    to break it,
He is not letting his allergies interfere with the mourning.

We sit like this until morning.

AS I LIKE AWAKE WITH HIM

Every short breath,
Every cloudy glance,
Every crushed pill
In peanut butter,

Studies
And examinations,
His kicking leg,

Stored away
Into the future,
Like the walks,

That pass through
The past without a word
Between us,
Hold on to him,

Watch his breaths,
See the moments
As his memory
Moves through time.

PRATTSBURG, SUMMER

The wild flowers
The winding winds thru turbines
The color of soap
The single market with its dollar meal wings
The hills that rise to the winds
The house like a dodecahedron
20 sides to every story
2 storeys high
Your quiet snore as you sleep on an air mattress on the
floor
The two floors, uneven like a prize fight
Awake into the night composing by firelight
As the logs decompose in amber
The redux of carbon and flame.
I will remember every frame of this day,
When we worked together to compensate
For the time we've spent apart
And to contemplate the many stories to come.

CROW HILL AUTUMN

Cold wind.
First snow of winter in October
Silent as crystals.
All that falls from above comes over
The north hill –
Bent and bruised poplars, beeches,
The weeds, Queen Anne's lace.
Apple trees.
Golden delicious sunlight glistens
Off their skins, delicate snow,
And I can only listen to the crisp crunch,
Biting into them the sound of snowfall.
The sunlight lingers on each flake
In a bed of reflection,
Like a winter lake sleeping.
Dormant is a long time
For each cotton stalk.
Songbirds are silent
On these days, reserved,
For a distant look
Into a life
Spilled on the road.

FRAMES

He reframed the basement,
Hung drywall when I was fourteen.
I sanded and painted with my father,
One of the few of his projects
Where he would let me lend a hand.

We were outsiders moving overseas,
But who isn't when they arrive,
With nothing but hold baggage and AAFES
To tide us over through the first winter
In the attic of the barracks.

The sixteen rooms dragged down the hall
Like a portal to Narnia or Dachau,
A lone mirror at the far end staring back
Across my adolescent sea,
Beyond where I could see.

I held off until the end of high school,
Ensuring Cs on pop quizzes scribbled
On the planks, on the blackboard.
I had relied upon the eyes of others,
And the words of my mother.

My father reframed my life,
Taught me to spackle, sand, and paint
With that putty knife, brush, block
So well that not a nail would show,
Nor the cracks from stretches at my edges.

But no matter how much I worked,
No matter how much I tried,
I was never prepared for his departure,
Never got the answers to so many of life's questions,
And now I'll never know.

2010

PASSING ON

I used to think naiveté was a temporary condition,
One that would pass along to the younger generation
Like acid washed jeans or Stone Temple Pilots.
But just like those who still consider themselves
An alternative to the norm,
Just like all the different people,
While in fact they are the target demographic,
The one with extra money they should be saving,
With all the unfulfilled consumer dreams of childhood,
Toys they never had now sitting on shelves unopened,
While they while away their evenings in someone else's
worlds.

I used to think getting involved
was the best way to be informed,
Now I see it as a waste of time
woven in fleeting moments,
Like those that disappear
when the candidate you've chosen
Is defeated, or wins and then reverts to his childhood,
That upstairs bedroom where the afternoon light sets
aglow
The many trophies earned in competitive matches
That mean nothing once the ashes are spread,
Boxes of plastic sell for 25 cents at the estate sale.
Maryland was so arbitrary,
and I never understood.
There is no place like home,
and it's all as it should.

So I am passing on this,
giving it back,
going away for awhile,
A stint abroad in a place
you will never know,
like your child.

THE LAST TIME

The last time I touched my father
Was as one end of a fireman's carry
Out from the master bedroom
For one last look at the setting sun.

He left me his whole name,
There was something distinct about it.
Out from under the second moniker
I could never blame him for it.

There was a hint of MacArthur,
In the smoky haze of history
I'm doomed to walk in his footsteps
Barely burdened by his load.

Death came for him on the solstice,
The longest day of the year,
On the longest of my life.

Each year in the receding shadow
Of his memory I'm reminded
Of how my mother kindly
Appeared peripheral in that light.

Under the shroud of night,
The moon the glint of a scythe
Flashed a lone utterance,
"I'll be back for another."

I walked out under the faint night sky
Of St. Michaels,

A town saved from the British,
Revered by the locals
In that colonial reverence.

Reconsidered the frontier,
Trot sprinted to run away
And still on to this day,
In search of the right space,
Unwilling to simply keep pace.

2011

NEWS

Someone once said
That somewhere in the world
Something is happening
And this something
Will make its way here.

I say that El Niño and La Niña
Are fucking in the basement
While the pure white clothes
Their mother has hung out to dry
Dance in the solar winds.

No amount of HIV or Ebola
Will stem the rising tides
Of piracy, iconoclasm, heresy,
Rocking through the trumpets
That once grew on the Horn.

Still men war over oil and water,
Medicine, wood, information
Changing minds over and over again
In ever-growing obituaries
Where something is happening.

BUILDUP

we walked through fits
with our fingers and thumbs
history our home

leaves and sticks
stones on stones

palms, knuckles, joints
ironing linens

found trust in a ring
of fists and hope
firing blazes
in cold cinder
dreams dust in ash
flint, iron and bone.

SHADOWS BY LAMPLIGHT

Shadows by lamplight
dance in the orange night
that drapes the strange flight
of windchimes.

Your Fulbright blocks the window
from your snare's neighborhood,
pale reminder of what you could
otherwise be doing,

who you would otherwise by helping
if not for the lure of the letters,
those three lonely letters
like some forgotten operetta.

Shadows by lamplight
dance in the moonlight,
warm glow of lumber mills
that bleach the paper

that fades the page
from the electronic age
of social anxieties
mediated by a thousand line virus.

Your shadow is fading
with each step you take
closer to him and up and away
from your mother.

HIGHWAY 17

Stealing time, pedal to the pavement
Saturday blitz through Santa Cruz hills
race to hit beach, see the waves
be the way that you want to behave
trying to save every penny to the grave
to earn that wage and not be a slave.
But it's Saturday and you want to get away
leave troubles behind for some other day
flying four wheels down that windy, narrow road.
Highway 17 is about to explode
with a flurry of drivers trying to get by
without a worry in their minds or a twinkle in their eyes.
I'm in a line that's moving way too fast
knowing all along this day will never last
I'm keeping my speed not letting anyone past.
Wrestling youth to chase down thrills
thinking of you, time to make a payment
Stolen time, pedal to the pavement.

BETWEEN THE SCALES & BONES

Again, I fly back to Maryland.
Sometimes out of the sky an idea arrives
In a phrase that falls from a cloud
That precipitates a meal of letters & words,
Cast from a line on the shore
A day or two before.
Between the scales & bones,
What do I say when the day is in motion
That would not cause a stink & commotion?

ESTUARY

One simple range.
Once would be enough,
A rock cast through a window
To convince us we are here.
Between the daily bread of the baker's kiln
And the ink that runs between fingers and lips
Stained with this morning's coffee.

Letters in an offset grid cast the grim shadows
Of a million summers. The air
As still as biology during a midterm.
Cursives overlap in scribbled pens,
Opportunity wanders in the margins.

Oxbow winds the land through time,
The endless meander of erosion,
Unabridged.

Repetition is a killer of words,
Seeks the destruction of a poem,
A sardonic moon, automated process,
Sublimated by the morning's deadline.

I too abhor the dull routine of existence,
The rise and shine, snide remarks of dawn.
Yet, in this marked passage there is silt
That wraps the printed page in a quilt

Folded over and over.

CYBO (DEATH BY TRANSLATION)

no hoba zoguna
pagzosgam ce new.
anonska kapmuna:
moves anna u ckpek.

nosvobwamo cubo.
news vew om cepebpo.
nemamno kupacubo.
no pub ugo go bpo.

none vloma
zumaga bewe gowva!
a mo kakbo uma?
cukpekeu u mosva.

MORTE

For E.A. Poe on the occasion of his birthday

Death comes quickly, leaves you on your back,
whether by seizure, aneurism, heart attack.
Death warms over like a father's cold hands,
a long walk in the woods til you've made amends.

Death steals what only thieves understand,
takes all life, all contraband
and in the lonely quiet of a clearing,
judges, first by sight, then by hearing.

Death has shallow migratory patterns,
causes migraines with twists and turns
down narrow alleys and busy streets,
strikes up a match with everyone.

Death breaks a rhyme, puts time on hold,
grinds the sinews and ends the old,
loosens up a tight poet's verse,
takes back every moment in the universe.

Stephen D. Hilderbrand is a data scientist, poet, linguist, photographer, storyteller, juggler, musician, father, friend, and husband living in Austin, TX. On occasion, he finds moments of solitude to write poems.

Written over five years of his life, *Already There* is a collection of thirty-two poems around the subject of searching for home. From St. Lucia to Maryland, to upstate New York, to Austin, he walks us through a real and imagined past in the hope of settling down amidst dense lines and rhyming meditation.

This book is the first poetry collection he has published with Inverspace Press.

www.ingramcontent.com/pod-product-compliance
Ingram Content Group UK Ltd.
Pitfield, Milton Keynes, MK11 3LW, UK
UKHW020216250726
13967UKWH00001B/26

9 781300 262442